D0850794

Shaquille O'Neal

Gentle Giant

Shaquille O'Neal

Gentle Giant

John Albert Torres

Enslow Publishers, Inc.

40 Industrial Road   PO Box 38
Box 398   Aldershot
Berkeley Heights, NJ 07922   Hants GU12 6BP
USA   UK

http://www.enslow.com

Library of Congress Cataloging-in-Publication Data

Torres, John Albert.
    Shaquille O'Neal : gentle giant / John Albert Torres.
       p. cm. — (Sports leaders series)
    Summary: Discusses the personal life and basketball career of the star center for the Los Angeles Lakers, Shaquille O'Neal.
    Includes bibliographical references and index.
    ISBN 0-7660-2175-0
    1. O'Neal, Shaquille—Juvenile literature. 2. Basketball players—United States—Biography—Juvenile literature. [1. O'Neal, Shaquille. 2. Basketball players. 3. African Americans—Biography.]
I. Title. II. Series.
GV884.O54T67 2004
796.323'092—dc21

                                        2003001282

Printed in the United States of America

10 9 8 7 6 5 4

To Our Readers: We have done our best to make sure all Internet Addresses in this book were active and appropriate when we went to press. However, the author and the publisher have no control over and assume no liability for the material available on those Internet sites or on other Web sites they may link to. Any comments or suggestions can be sent by e-mail to comments@enslow.com or to the address on the back cover.

Illustration Credits: ALLSPORT USA/Allsport, p. 65; Brad Messina/LSU, pp. 48, 53; Donald Miralle/ALLSPORT, p. 84; Elsa Hasch/ALLSPORT, p. 37; Enslow Publishers, Inc., p. 77; Ezra O. Shaw/ALLSPORT, p. 80; Fernando Medina/NBAE/Getty Images, p. 91; Jed Jacobsohn/ALLSPORT, pp. 29, 32, 41; Jeff Gross/ALLSPORT, pp. 17, 20; Jeff Gross/Getty Images, p. 58; Jonathan Daniel/ALLSPORT, pp. 6, 68, 70; Lisa Blumenfeld/Getty Images, pp. 74, 89; Mike Cooper/ALLSPORT, p. 63; Mike Powell/Getty Images, p. 72; Nathaniel S. Butler/NBAE/Getty Images, p. 93; Otto Greule/ALLSPORT, p. 87; Phil Sears/ALLSPORT, p. 50; Tim DeFrisco/ALLSPORT, pp. 11, 14, 24, 26.

Cover Illustration: Andrew D. Bernstein / NBAE via Getty Images.

CONTENTS

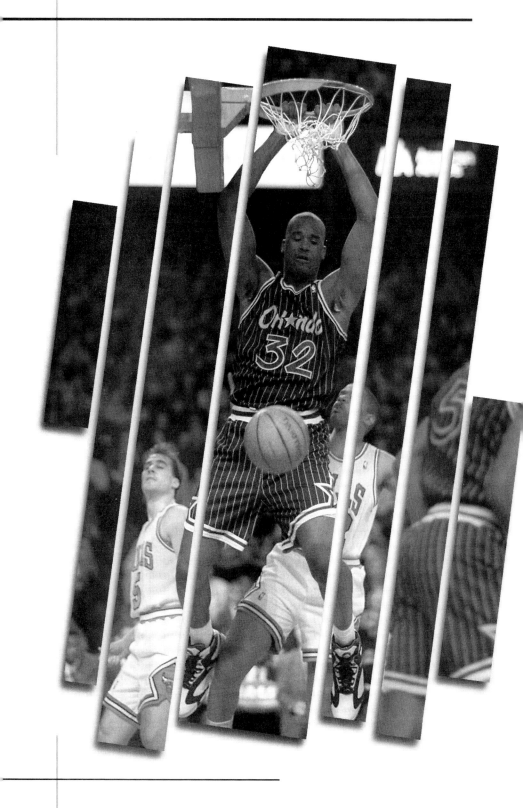

1

NO
PRESSURE
AT ALL

Rarely before had the National Basketball Association (NBA) and its fans waited with such eager anticipation for a rookie player to take the court for the first time. Sure, there was quite a buzz when Hall-of-Famers Bill Walton, Wilt Chamberlain, and Kareem Abdul-Jabbar first stepped on the hardwood of an NBA arena, but this seemed like much, much more. Throughout the summer of 1992, newspapers and sports highlight shows were speculating about whether Shaquille O'Neal, the powerhouse from Louisiana State University, would live up to the hype.

Shaquille, only twenty years old, had been steady

but unspectacular during the short exhibition season for the Orlando Magic. He averaged just under 20 points a game and had grabbed his share of rebounds—but it was still only the preseason. How would Shaq, as he was already known, do when the games really counted? How would he do with just about the whole world watching his NBA debut? How would he react to the pressure?

> **Would Shaquille O'Neal, the powerhouse from Louisiana State University, live up to the hype?**

For the wide-smiled giant, there was no pressure at all.

"I have no expectations," he said before his first game as a professional. "I like to experience things for myself. I don't believe in pressure. I don't worry about anything. I'm too young to worry." But then Shaq lost the big smile for a moment as his words took a more serious tone. "I know there are a lot of expectations for me to become great. If I do become a great center like Chamberlain, [Bill] Russell, or Kareem, that's good. If not, I'll live a happy life and keep on smiling."[1]

But many knew that Shaq's smile would not last long if he did not live up to the hype and promise that made him the richest rookie player ever. There were a lot of people counting on Shaq to become the dominant center they felt he could be. Even the city where he would be playing was hoping for big things from the "big kid."

Orlando, Florida, already known for its famous theme parks and recognizable names like Mickey Mouse and Shamu, was hoping that Shaquille O'Neal would prove to be one more attraction luring people to central Florida. After all, the Magic had never been a winning franchise in its short history and had never really developed a personality, except for being the only team in the league to wear black pinstripes. The basketball fans in the region were starving for something to cheer for, they were looking for a hero. The Magic had been in existence for three seasons and had posted a 70–176 record—not much to cheer about.

But the night that the Magic won the draft lottery and the rights to select first in the NBA draft, everyone knew the team would be picking Shaquille O'Neal. After all, every representative from the eleven lottery teams had a special jersey made up with O'Neal written across the back just in case they were awarded the first pick. Ten of them went home disappointed. Pat Williams, general manager for the Magic, gleefully held up the O'Neal jersey he had made up and called the team to open the ticket window. Fifty fans bought season tickets that very night. That week a hundred more fans bought season tickets. There was finally some hope, a dominant center that the young team could build its franchise around. Overnight the Magic had gone from a doormat team to a serious playoff contender.

When the Magic drafted Shaq, the fans instantly began calling him the savior who would bring a championship to Orlando. That was only a part of the pressure that was placed on Shaq's shoulders. The NBA also was looking for another star to market. After years of bad publicity, the NBA was winning back its fans, mainly on the strength of legendary scorer Michael Jordan. So the NBA was hoping that Shaq would follow in Jordan's footsteps—someone who would appeal to the serious basketball fan as well as the little kids. There were a lot of eyes on Shaq.

Even the marketing people were counting on O'Neal capturing the attention of the nation. Before he was due to attend training camp with the rest of his teammates, he flew to Las Vegas to film a television commercial with legendary college coach John Wooden and Hall-of-Fame basketball centers Bill Russell, Kareem Abdul-Jabbar, and Bill Walton. Here was this twenty-year-old kid who was already being

*Shaquille O'Neal faced enormous media pressure before taking
the court in his first game for the Orlando Magic in 1992.*

spoken about in the same breath and appearing in television commercials with some of the greatest players in history. He had signed an incredible endorsement deal with Reebok, a sneaker company that was counting on the giant with the big smile to help them sell athletic apparel. Even before he scored one NBA point, Shaq was becoming a household name. It is truly astonishing that Shaq was able to handle the hype and the pressure as well as he did.

On opening night of the 1992–93 season, the capacity crowd of 15,151 at the Orlando O-Rena went wild when Shaq took the court for his pre-game warm-ups. The hysteria lasted right on through to the opening tip, which Shaq controlled against Miami Heat center Rony Seikaly. There were reporters and television crews on hand from all over the United States, as well as from basketball-hungry countries in South America, Japan, Spain, and France. In all there were about 180 reporters present. The world was interested to see how this much-hyped basketball player would do in his first game. The game had taken on a playoff-like atmosphere.

Shaq disappointed no one.

He took control of the game early with his own special brand of power basketball, from thundering slam dunks to pulling down rebound after rebound.

The big trademark smile was gone and Shaq had on his "game face." He was once described by NBA coach George Karl as having a real killer instinct in his eyes. Shaq loved to smile and have a good time, but once he stepped on to the basketball court he was all about playing hard and trying to win. He was all business.

Shaq saved his best work for the second half. With the Magic working to erase a 10-point halftime deficit, Shaq showed the hometown fans just what they could expect to see all season long with a pair of astonishing back-to-back plays that had fans rocking the arena and the Miami Heat players shaking their heads.

> **"I have no expectations. . . . I don't believe in pressure. I don't worry about anything."**
> **—Shaquille O'Neal**

Both plays started with Shaq's strength: his incredible ability to rebound a missed shot. Shaq grabbed the rebound from the glass and dribbled the ball the length of the court. He was so fast that no one could catch him. It is not every day that you see a seven-footer dribble a basketball from "coast to coast." But Shaq did just that, ending the play with a monstrous slam dunk that left the backboard shaking. The fans were still in awe from the first play

Shaquille O'Neal looks to shoot during a game against the Denver Nuggets in 1992.

when he grabbed the next rebound on the defensive end and, seeing no one in front of him, decided to dribble the length of the court again! This time, instead of treating the fans to another rim-rocking, two-handed jam, he showed fans and teammates alike that he was more than a slam dunk.

Just as fans and players alike thought Shaq was driving in for another dunk, he showed his generous spirit by dishing the ball off to teammate Anthony Bowie at the last second for an easy layup. It was a beautiful assist for O'Neal, and the crowd once again went wild. It felt as if the arena itself was shaking on its foundations. This was a feeling Shaq would have to get used to in a hurry.

Almost as impressive was Shaq's play during the Magic's run to start the fourth quarter. Looking a lot like an experienced Bill Russell or Bill Walton, Shaq dominated the paint area and closed the lanes to passes and would-be scorers as the Magic held the Heat without a field goal for the first eight minutes of the quarter. He also made sure the Heat did not get any second chance opportunities at the basket by snatching every rebound and loose ball he could reach. The Magic outscored their cross-state rivals 29–19 during that stretch to take a commanding lead, which they held onto, winning 110–100.

After the game reporters and teammates alike could not stop talking about those two plays Shaq had made. Some even kidded him that he looked like an experienced NBA point guard on those two plays. In basketball, the point guard is the player who normally dribbles the ball up court. Rarely do you see a center do it.

"If I'm able to do it then I'll do it," Shaq grinned. "I mean it's a lot of fun. Most big guys don't do that." Shaq spent a lot more time talking about the brilliant pass he had made to Bowie instead of the 12 points he scored himself. "We had a three-on-one break and I acted like I was going to pass to Dennis Scott. Then I saw a white jersey out of the side of my eye and I passed to Anthony Bowie for the layup."[2]

In addition to the 12 points and the victory, Shaq had 3 blocked shots, 2 assists, and an astonishing 18 rebounds—this despite playing only 32 minutes because of foul trouble. (In the NBA, a player fouls out of a game by committing six fouls. A player is said to be in "foul trouble" when he has four or five fouls in the game or three already in the first half.) The 18 boards were the most for a rookie in his debut since Bill Walton played his first game in 1974 with the Portland Trail Blazers—not bad company at all.

Shaquille O'Neal prepares to take a free throw. O'Neal had to work very hard to improve his free throw shooting early on in his pro career.

The rookie did make some mistakes, though: He committed eight turnovers and he was also called for some silly fouls. But after the game, Miami Heat center Rony Seikaly complimented Shaq by describing him as a "monster." Seikaly had also had problems guarding O'Neal during some exhibition games. The rookie had indeed arrived.

Just about everyone was amazed at Shaq's impressive start except for his teammates, who had seen how hard the rookie worked at his game every day in the gym. Shaq was one of the first to show up for practice and one of the last players to leave. He would watch videos and work on things he had learned in basketball camps and clinics over the years. Teammate and close friend Dennis Scott said it was obvious right from the start that Shaq wanted to get better and better every time he walked onto the basketball court.

Shaquille O'Neal had arrived and was at the doorstep of NBA stardom. Over his next few seasons in Orlando, Shaq would help make the Magic into a major force in the NBA. Before long, he was leading Orlando in some classic match-ups against Michael Jordan and the Chicago Bulls in the Eastern Conference playoffs, as well as Hakeem Olajuwon and the Houston Rockets in the NBA Finals.

Then in 1996, Shaq left Orlando as a free agent and signed with the Los Angeles Lakers. With the Lakers, O'Neal truly came into his own as a player, winning three championships in a row between 2000 and 2002. Looking back on that commercial he did as a rookie with all of those legendary NBA centers, one could argue that Shaq has turned out to be the greatest of them all.

Shaquille O'Neal's long climb up the ladder of athletic success is truly an amazing story. It had been a long journey from humble beginnings that started in 1972.

2

LITTLE
WARRIOR

Shaquille Rashaun O'Neal was born on March 6, 1972, in a poor neighborhood in Newark, New Jersey. Shaq was an average size and weight when he was born, weighing in at seven pounds, eleven ounces. It was probably the only time in his life that he was actually small! Being born poor was only one of the many obstacles Shaquille would have to overcome in his early years. His mother, Lucille O'Neal, had recently finished high school and was living in a low-income housing project when Shaquille was born. Her neighborhood was primarily African American and there was a large concentration of black Muslims. Even though Lucille was not a Muslim, many of her friends were. She decided to look at a book of Islamic names when she found out she was having a baby. Two of the names struck her instantly: Shaquille Rashaun. She loved the two names because they mean "Little Warrior."

Shaquille's father left Lucille even before Shaquille was born, so Shaq never got a chance to know his biological dad. Luckily for Shaquille, his mother married Philip Harrison. The newlyweds decided to let Shaquille keep his mother's name because there were no other boys in her family to carry on the family name. Both Lucille and Philip worked for the city of Newark, which just a few years earlier had been the scene of very bad race riots in which many people had gotten hurt and fires had burned down many buildings.

Things got bad for the city government and there was little opportunity for Harrison to advance and pull his family out of poverty. For a while, he even worked three jobs at once, trying to do the most for his wife and son. Harrison drove trucks, shined shoes, and sold hats. He did whatever it would take to keep his family above the poverty line. Eventually, Harrison decided to join the U.S. Army. At least in the army Harrison knew he would be able to advance and there was also job security.

When Shaquille was five years old, his little sister was born. Her parents named her Lateefah, another Muslim name. The couple had another girl when Shaquille was six and named her Ayesha. Finally, a little brother, Jamal, was born the following year. The family was growing fast.

As a little boy, Shaq was always getting himself into mischief. His grandmother, as well as his mom and dad, would always have to watch him closely. The minute they turned their backs Shaq was off to find some other adventure. It was during this time that Shaq developed a very close relationship with his grandmother.

The army did provide for a way out of the Newark ghettos.

When Shaquille O'Neal was born he weighed seven pounds, eleven ounces.

The family soon moved to an army base in Bayonne, New Jersey. This is where Shaquille and his siblings learned about life as an "army brat"—a term given to children of career soldiers in the army.

That was also where they learned what a strict disciplinarian their dad, Philip Harrison, could be. Harrison would let the kids know when they had done something wrong and he let them have it if

Growing up, Shaquille O'Neal spent a great deal of time with his grandmother, with whom he enjoyed a strong relationship.

they did not cooperate. To Harrison, the idea of being a strict father made a lot of sense.

"I was running wild and playing ball," Philip Harrison said, explaining how he misspent his childhood and didn't listen to his own father. "I didn't realize what he was saying until I had my own children."[1]

Sometimes Shaquille did not understand why his father needed to be so tough with him. It would only be much later when he realized just how important it was for him to be disciplined.

Harrison wanted Shaquille to be the first child in his or his wife's family to go to college, so at times he was extra hard on Shaquille. He did not stand for any behavior problems from the little warrior.

Sometimes Shaquille thought that his father did not love him and he would complain to his mother. But she told Shaquille not to listen to the way his father reacted but instead to listen to the things he said. Her words made a lot of sense and it would later dawn on Shaquille that his dad only wanted the best for him. "Thank goodness I had two parents that loved me enough to stay on my case," Shaq would later say as an adult.[2]

Perhaps the most difficult thing about growing up as an army brat was the constant moving. Even

By the time he was thirteen years old, Shaq already wore a size seventeen sneaker. Today, he wears a size twenty-two.

Shaq's first move to the army base in Bayonne was a tough one for him. Shaq was very close to his grandmother and did not want to leave her. Because both of his parents worked, for a while she had a very big role in raising the youngster.

But Harrison's new position as a staff sergeant meant that he needed to spend a lot more time on the base. It made sense for him to want his family nearby. Plus, it was a way to get better housing and a better education for his kids.

As a child Shaq was always big for his age. He grew much faster than the other children and sometimes he had a hard time making friends. Many times the other kids would be afraid because Shaq was so big. They thought he would be mean so they shied away from him. Sometimes kids would even make fun of his different name. Shaquille would sometimes get embarrassed of his height and slouch down. His parents would yell at him to be proud of who he was and to stand tall. But Shaquille did not listen. He just wanted to fit in with the other kids. He wanted to be "normal." Because he was so tall Shaquille was not very graceful. In fact, he was very clumsy and the kids would tease him constantly.

Shaq used to get into a lot of fights at school. He would get tired of the other kids teasing him or he would constantly be challenged by kids who wanted to prove how tough they were by fighting with him.

It was also hard on Shaquille because the family was constantly on the move with the army. Every time Harrison was assigned to another army base, the family would have to pick up and move wherever he was sent. Looking back, Shaq said that those years were probably the hardest of his life. Despite his big family, Shaq was lonely. He said that the family moved around so much that he never even got to have a best friend.

But that moving around also helped make Shaquille tougher. It made him learn to accept new surroundings and new people and ideas. It made him learn to adapt to different things all the time. It also helped to make him more independent.

One thing that was constant wherever they moved, however, was sports, and Shaquille began to love sports at a very young age. His fast-growing body made him a little too awkward for baseball but in football and basketball it is good if you are big. So that's exactly what he played: football and basketball.

As a nine year old Shaquille got his first taste of organized sports when his father signed him up in a youth basketball league. By this time the family was living at an army base in Georgia known as Fort Stewart, and Shaquille was much bigger than the other kids. His father, a former junior college basketball star himself, was Shaquille's first coach. Even to this day Shaquille credits his dad with teaching him the fundamentals of the game of basketball. In fact, whenever Shaq is having a hard time, he will call Harrison and ask him for advice.

Harrison was a Boston Celtics fan. He liked to

Shaq is congratulated by his father, Philip Harrison, on the court after a game. Shaq credits his father's discipline for leading to much of the success he enjoys today as an NBA star.

brag that former Boston Celtic superstar Dave Cowens had once accidentally knocked out his teeth during a pickup basketball game in East Orange, New Jersey. Harrison would often teach the Celtics' plays to the youth basketball team. The Celtics were always known as a solid fundamental basketball team that stressed teamwork and passing. It was a good foundation for Shaquille and the other children to learn.

> "Thank goodness I had two parents that loved me enough to stay on my case."
>
> —Shaquille O'Neal

As a coach Harrison tried to instill a winning attitude in Shaq. He wanted him to play his best and his hardest every time he stepped out on the floor. Sometimes Shaquille found it hard to live up to his dad's expectations. His dad would bark orders at him from across the basketball court.

"The world has too many followers and not enough leaders," Harrison would tell his son.[3] He wanted Shaquille to be a leader on the court and off.

Of course, Shaq was still only nine years old. By this time, he had lost interest in becoming a basketball player and had decided he wanted to be a dancer, instead. Shaq used to watch dance shows on television and would imitate the moves he saw. This was when break dancing was very popular. He taught himself a lot of dance steps. Shaq would spin and slide on big pieces of cardboard, perfecting his moves. When the television show *Fame* aired, Shaquille was hooked. He worked hard at the dance moves and was sure he was going to be a dancer.

Shaq credits his mother's gracefulness as the reason why he became such a good dancer. His parents were proud of him. Dancing was safe, they thought, and it would help keep Shaq out of trouble.

Shaquille used to also spend a lot of his time watching martial arts movies. He loved watching people do karate and kung fu and he would sometimes imitate those moves, too. Hall-of-Fame basketball player Kareem Abdul-Jabbar was also a lover of martial arts and was even taught karate by legendary martial artist Bruce Lee.

Of course, fate and his increasing body size would have something different in store for Shaquille.

A BASKETBALL FUTURE

As Shaquille continued to grow, it became apparent that he just might have a future playing basketball. In fact, his father would sometimes joke with Shaquille by throwing him a basketball and telling him that it was going to help him make a lot of money some day.

It was not until something happened while playing his other favorite sport—football—that Shaq decided to really start playing basketball full time. As a young teenager, he was living on an army base in Wildeflecken in what was then West Germany. During a football game with other soldiers' children Shaq was tackled and did not like the feeling.

"I might not have played basketball, except that one of those little muscular guys tackled me in the knee," Shaq said.[1] After hurting his knee Shaq decided that it would be a lot safer—and he could last a lot longer—playing basketball.

Shaquille was already six feet six inches tall at the age of thirteen. When the pain in his knee did not go away, Shaquille underwent a physical examination. He was found to have Osgood-Schlatter disease, an affliction that affects bone structure. It is not uncommon in growing young boys. Shaq was forced to rest a lot as well as drink a lot of milk to make his bones stronger by giving them calcium. It was official. Football was out and as soon as he felt better, basketball would be it for him.

But just because he was tall, Shaq was by no means a natural on the basketball court. In fact, he was pretty lousy. Shaq could not jump very high, was very clumsy, could not dribble, could not catch a pass, and was a lousy shooter. His success today is a testament to how hard Shaquille worked to make himself into a superstar. O'Neal has said that God only gave him 48 percent of his athletic ability; the other 52 percent was the result of hard work.

Sometimes Shaquille would grow frustrated. Expectations were very high on him because of his height. He would get upset when he did not improve the way he thought he should. But he never gave up. His dad would always explain to his son how hard work would one day pay off. Slowly but surely, Shaquille did begin to improve.

Even though he started to love the game of basketball, Shaquille hated living on the army base in Germany. He wanted to go back to the United States. He thought that if he misbehaved his parents would send him back home to live with his grandmother. He was wrong. It only made his parents angry at him and his father even paddled Shaq in front of his friends after he had done something wrong.

That's when the youngster realized that he could stay out of trouble by playing basketball. He decided to give up the mischief and start concentrating on the game. But

> **O'Neal has said that God only gave him 48 percent of his athletic ability; the other 52 percent was the result of hard work.**

Shaq was served another disappointment when as a high school freshman he failed to make the school's basketball team. The army base had its own schools and even though he was the tallest kid on the base, Shaq simply was not good enough.

Fate would step in, however. Dale Brown, the

legendary successful basketball coach for Louisiana State University (LSU), was on a tour of military bases throughout Europe to give free basketball clinics. One of his stops was the base in Wildeflecken, where Shaq's dad was stationed.

Shaquille was still discouraged by not making the school's team when his father talked him into going to the clinic. Shaq had never heard of Brown but decided to go and see if there was something he could learn. He was hoping that Brown could help him to increase his jumping abilities.

In what is now a rather famous story, Brown began talking about basketball with Shaquille at the clinic when he asked "the soldier" how long he had been in the army. Shaq replied that he was only thirteen years old! Brown could not believe it—his jaw nearly hit the ground. He started thinking four years down the line and how nice it would be to have a player as big as Shaq on his college team. He knew that Shaquille would continue to grow.

The two hit it off right away, and Brown even made friends with Shaquille's father. He gave Shaq a good exercise program that would help Shaq strengthen his legs. Brown's jaw hit the ground again when he learned that Shaq did not even make the school's basketball team.

Dale Brown (above), head coach of men's basketball at Louisiana State University, first met Shaquille O'Neal at a basketball clinic in Germany in 1985. Although O'Neal was just thirteen, he was so tall that Brown mistook him for an adult.

O'Neal would never get another chance to try out for the team. His father was transferred again, this time back to the United States, to an army base in San Antonio, Texas.

Shaq had worked hard on the strengthening programs that Brown had suggested, and he and his father continued working hard to develop skills on the basketball court. This time, when Shaq tried out for his new school's basketball team, he knew it would be a different story.

In fact, when Cole High School's basketball coaches first saw Shaquille, they could not believe it. They knew right away that Shaq could form the nucleus of a championship-caliber basketball team. Shaquille was six feet ten inches tall by this time! That is the size of some NBA centers.

"O'Neal was like a pot of gold being dropped from the sky," said Head Coach Dave Madura. "Coaching him was the highlight of my life. There was no doubt that he was going to be a big-time player. But he never flaunted it."[2]

What also impressed the small school's coaching staff was how well-behaved and respectful a teenager Shaquille was. All those years of his father's strict discipline had paid off.

Years later, Shaq would look back and comment

on how athletes did not make good role models, especially when two bona fide role models were available every day.

"My mother and father were my real role models," Shaq would say. "I used to like Dr. J [basketball legend Julius Irving], but I couldn't talk to Dr. J about the birds and the bees. . . . We don't know a lot about these people [celebrities]; parents should teach their kids to emulate someone who's positive and well-rounded."[3]

Shaq became a team leader on the court, especially in practice where he worked hard. His basketball skills had increased tremendously. He was gaining weight and becoming stronger, especially in his lower body and legs. Pretty soon he had no trouble at all dunking the basketball and would sometimes wow his teammates in practice with spectacular types of dunks.

> "My mother and father were my real role models."
>
> —Shaquille O'Neal

The team brought in a former player at the school, the six-foot six-inch Herb More. His job was to work primarily with Shaq every single day. More joked that his job was to hang onto Shaquille so that he could dunk the ball with a little opposition in his way. More would later become the head coach at Cole High after Madura retired.

Shaquille's newfound dunking abilities caused some controversy throughout the high school league. Shaq would dunk the ball so hard through the rim that he sometimes would bend the rims on opposing courts. In a game against rival Southside High School, Shaq's thunderous dunks caused one of the rims to bend in three places. After the game was over it looked as if a monster had toyed with the metal rim.

Opposing schools got angry with Cole because they thought Shaq was hanging onto the rims and bending them on purpose. But they soon realized that was not the case. The truth was that Shaquille would dunk the ball with such ferocity that it would cause the rims to become misshapen. Soon the other schools began to replace their rims with collapsible baskets to prevent Shaquille from bending any more rims.

Before Shaquille's junior season, Coach Madura told his squad that anything but a state championship would be unacceptable. After all, there was nobody in the league that could stop Shaquille.

The team cruised to an undefeated regular season and Shaquille was starting to enjoy the newfound celebrity status that had started to follow him. His highlights would make local sports broadcasts

Shaq hangs on to the rim after dunking the ball during a playoff game in 2001. While playing high school ball, some rival schools replaced their normal baskets with collapsible ones to keep Shaq from bending their rims.

and his reputation as a dunking machine grew. Unfortunately for Shaq and his teammates, they started talking the talk before walking the walk.

Just before the state championship game Shaquille told local television stations that he guaranteed he would score 50 points and that there was "nobody on earth" who could stop him. Shaquille was especially confident because the opposing center, for Liberty Hill High School, was only six feet three inches tall. But Shaquille found himself in foul trouble early in the game and had to sit out most of the first half. Soon, his team was down 21–2. He scored only 8 points, but the team got back into the game and was involved in a back and forth duel with their underdog opponents. With five seconds left to play, Shaquille was fouled with his team down by only one point. This was his chance to be a hero.

"People were screaming and shouting," Shaq recalled. "I missed the first one and then missed the second one and that was the game. That was the last time I ever said that I was [better] than anyone."[4]

That bad experience proved to be a good lesson for Shaquille and his teammates. When senior year rolled around the boys were more determined than ever to win the state crown. Once again they breezed through the regular season, going an astonishing

36–0! Shaq obviously led the team in most categories including averaging 32.1 points, 22 rebounds, and 8 blocked shots per game.

In one memorable game, Shaq scored 27 points and grabbed a whopping 36 rebounds and 26 blocked shots! To put it into perspective, a player is normally congratulated after grabbing 15 rebounds and blocking four or five shots.

This time the team did little talking and disposed of opponents in the state tournament, easily winning the state crown. This was quite an accomplishment for Shaquille because for the entire season he was being heavily recruited and watched by just about every major college with a basketball program in America. Shaq was, by far, the most wanted high school basketball player in the country.

Shaquille began to enjoy the newfound celebrity status. . . . His highlights would make local sports broadcasts and his reputation as a dunking machine grew.

After the season, Shaq was invited to play in the High School All-America basketball game. This is an annual high school all-star game featuring the best players in the country. Shaq dominated the game by scoring 18 points and pulling down 16 rebounds. He was named one of the game's most valuable players.

Powerhouse programs like the University of Nevada-Las Vegas (UNLV); University of North Carolina; Louisville; North Carolina State; Kentucky; Duke; Indiana; and others sent coaches and mailed letters. But one coach's kindness a few years earlier at an army base in Germany was never forgotten. Despite his father's desire for his son to play at the University of North Carolina, Shaq preferred to play for Dale Brown at LSU, Louisiana State University.

So, in order to concentrate on basketball, Shaq ended speculation early and announced to the nation that he would be playing college basketball at LSU.

4

COLLEGE SUPERSTAR

Shaquille O'Neal did not become a college superstar right away. In fact, his first season at LSU was filled with difficult adjustments. One of those major adjustments was being away from his family. It was the first time that he had lived apart from his parents and siblings. On the weekends, Shaq would drive seven hours from Baton Rouge, Louisiana, to San Antonio, Texas, where his family still lived.

Of course, on weekends that Shaq had a game, his family would make the long drive in order to cheer him on. But Shaq learned right off the bat that playing for a major college was a lot different than playing against high school kids.

In high school, Shaq was usually much bigger than the other kids and could just power his way to a rebound or a slam dunk. Suddenly, the defenders in college were a lot taller, a lot stronger, and a lot quicker than the high school kids. Another thing that weighed on Shaq's mind was being able to live up to the hype. After all, he was the most celebrated high school player in the country, joining a team that boasted two stars in Chris Jackson and Stanley Roberts. One preseason magazine even predicted that LSU would win the national championship.

Shaquille O'Neal did not become a college superstar right away. In fact, his first season at LSU was filled with difficult adjustments.

Shaq quickly realized that if he wanted to succeed at this level he needed to work more at his game and get a lot stronger. He would spend hours in the weight room lifting weights. Sometimes he would work out for so long that his friends would have to help him back to his room because he was so tired.

As the season started, it was clear that LSU was not as good a team as people had predicted. They did not seem to play as a team and the offense was very predictable. Chris Jackson would take most of the team's shots and Shaq basically had to wait for a missed shot for a rebound to get his hands on the ball. This was a difficult adjustment for someone who had been used to being the center of attention.

"It was a very difficult year for me," Shaquille would later say. "The only time I got the ball was on rebounds. Most of my shots were fadeaways in the paint with a hand in my face."[1]

Shaq made the most of his opportunities and scored more than 20 points five times during the season. That's not bad for a freshman player! He also continued to work on the defensive end, grabbing rebounds and blocking shots. He finished the year with 115 blocked shots, setting a Southeastern Conference record. The LSU Tigers finished with a disappointing 23–9 record and were eliminated quickly from postseason tournaments.

Shaq averaged only 13.9 points per game but both Jackson and Roberts went to the NBA after the season, meaning Shaq would be the focal point of the offense for his sophomore year. This was when Coach Dale Brown really had to go to work, because most of Shaq's success in high school had come on the slam dunk. Brown found it hard to get Shaq to improve his offensive game. When Brown wanted Shaq to try a hook shot or a turnaround jump shot, the big center would simply try and dunk the ball.

Shaquille O'Neal and his college teammates receive instructions from Head Coach Dale Brown.

Brown even resorted to bringing in some former NBA legends, Kareem Abdul-Jabbar and Bill Walton, to work with Shaq. He listened and seemed to work at it, but then during the games he would resort to his dunking ways.

It was hard for Shaq to change because this was the style of basketball he was used to. Ever since he started playing the game, O'Neal had been taught by his dad to simply rely on his size and power.

"My father always taught me to go out there and show everyone that this is my court, this is my ball, so you'd better get out of the way," Shaq said.[2]

Eventually the coach and player compromised and Shaq began to score points like they both knew he could. During his sophomore season Shaq regularly scored more than 30 points a game and, in a December game against Arkansas State, he put on one of the most remarkable scoring displays of his career.

Shaq used an impressive amount of dunks, hooks, jump shots, and put-backs to score 53 of his team's 98 points by connecting on 18 baskets and 17 free throws. A poor free-throw shooter, Shaq missed only four that game as the Tigers cruised to an easy victory. He also worked hard on the defensive end, grabbing 18 rebounds.

Shaq dunks the ball during a game against the Florida Gators on February 27, 1991.

Shaq worked on other parts of his game that he was proud of, too. In one game he dribbled the length of the court on a fast break and even dribbled the ball behind his back. He was also quick to point out some of his better passes to reporters after the games.

Shaq suffered his first injury near the end of the season when he landed awkwardly after a play and fractured his leg. He would only miss a couple of games.

Unfortunately, the team finished with a 20–10 record and once again was shut out of any postseason championships. But despite the disappointments for the team, Shaq continued to improve as well as become a better person. Shaq became very popular around the college campus for his easy-going style, big smile, and all-around friendly nature. It seemed as if everyone who crossed Shaq's path came away with a kind word for the gentle giant.

"Shaquille is a very loving guy," Dale Brown would say shortly after Shaquille turned pro. "He's someone you always want to hug and he's always embracing others. The best part about Shaquille is the way he treats other people."[3]

A husband and wife in Louisiana named their newborn son after Shaquille. Shaq was so moved that he drove out to the couple's home to meet the baby and pose for pictures with him. It was things like that, as well as always being willing to sign autographs, that helped make Shaq such a popular player. Whenever Shaq gave an autograph, he would sign his name and then add the words "listen to your mother."

Shaq finished the season with a 27.6 scoring average and won several college awards, including United Press International and Associated Press Player of the Year. He was also voted college player of the year by *Sports Illustrated* and L.A. Gear. When Shaq was awarded the Tanqueray Amateur Athletic Achievement Award and an accompanying $5,000 prize. He donated the money to the Boys and Girls Club of Newark, New Jersey.

Some college coaches were already calling Shaq the best overall center in the country—including the NBA! "He's a combination of David Robinson and Hakeem Olajuwon," said NBA and college coaching great Rick Pitino. "He's 295 pounds of grace."[4]

Some people were trying to pressure Shaq to leave college early and start his career in the NBA. But Shaq's father assured him that the money would be there when he was ready to leave college. He wanted Shaq to get an education. By this time, Shaq had decided that he would major in business. He

Shaq stands at the foul line and waits to receive the ball from the ref before attempting a free throw.

wanted a career to fall back on in case his NBA career did not pan out.

For now, the NBA would wait. Shaq decided to stay in school and continue playing for LSU. During the summer Shaq worked hard on his ball-handling skills, as well as his outside shooting. Shaq knew that if he wanted to one day play in the NBA he would not be able to rely solely on dunking the basketball. After all, just about everyone in the NBA can dunk the ball.

> "The best part about Shaquille is the way he treats other people."
>
> —Dale Brown

Coach Brown was impressed with how much Shaq had improved during the off-season. But it would be another frustrating season for LSU and Shaq. The team had gotten significantly weaker for Shaq's third year there. There was no one on the team who could consistently hit a jump shot. This makes things much harder for a high-scoring center like Shaq. Because opposing teams do not have to worry about an outside shooter scoring points against them, they were able to double and triple team Shaquille every time he got the ball.

Sometimes Shaq would even be surrounded by four players when he caught the ball. He also felt that teams had begun fouling him and playing very rough against him. This did not bother Shaq except that he felt he was not getting the foul calls. He started complaining that opposing players were pulling on his jersey or pushing him in the back every time he touched the ball.

It started to affect his play. Some critics said that Shaq started to just go through the motions. They said that he seemed as if he was playing not to get hurt, so that he could have an NBA career. The team got off to a slow start and Shaq's family served as his biggest critics. His father told him that he was "playing too nice." Even Shaq's grandmother told him that she noticed a big difference in his play from his sophomore season to his junior year. That's when Shaq said he woke up and started playing even harder. That's when the Tigers started posting victories.

The team rattled off seven straight wins and 10 of the next 11. The Tigers finished with a 19–8 record and a genuine chance to win the SEC Championship. But in the team's first-round game against rival Tennessee, Shaq was fouled hard by Carlus Groves and he turned around swinging. Even though Shaq had learned as a kid that it was better to walk away from a fight, he was sick and tired of the hard fouls. He was thrown out of the game and suspended for the next one.

"After that game, I made up my mind to enter the NBA draft,"[5] a frustrated Shaq said. His father wanted him to stay in school but his mother told her son that it was his decision to make.

Shaquille did not tell anybody about his NBA plans yet. He still hoped to lead LSU to an NCAA Tournament Championship. In the first game, Shaquille was a record-breaking defensive force. He blocked 11 shots, a record, sending many of them several rows deep into the stands. He also scored 26 points and grabbed 13 boards, leading the Tigers to a 94–83 victory.

> "He's a combination of David Robinson and Hakeem Olajuwon. He's 295 pounds of grace."
>
> —Rick Pitino on Shaquille O'Neal

If the Tigers could beat top-rated Indiana in the next round then they would have a serious shot at winning the tournament. Shaq was determined to play the game of his life. Before the contest started, he laid down in the locker room and listened to rap music with headphones on in order to psyche himself up. He knew the game might be his last college game and he wanted to play his heart out.

And play he did. He scored 36 points, many on thunderous slam dunks, grabbed 12 rebounds, and blocked 5 shots. But it was not enough. The Hoosiers ended LSU's season, 89–79.

A few weeks later, Shaquille held a press conference to let the world know that he would be leaving college early to play in the NBA. He promised his mother that he would continue to take classes when he could and someday earn his degree.

Now it was time for NBA general managers to dream about getting Shaquille and time for Shaquille to start some dreams of his own. He told friends that as excited as he was about going to the NBA, he was even more excited that he would be able to buy his mother the house she always wanted.

NBA
STARDOM

N ot many players in the history of the NBA enjoyed the quick success and immense popularity that accompanied Shaquille O'Neal when he became an instant star with the Orlando Magic.

Sure, he still had flaws in his game. He was clumsy at times and was a terrible free-throw shooter, but his hustle, style, and big grin endeared him to basketball fans across the globe. Of course, it also helped that in his first year as a member of the Orlando Magic, O'Neal proved himself to be one of the best centers in the NBA. He also made everyone else around him better—the mark of a true superstar.

In fact, just one month into his rookie season, the

Magic posted an 8–3 record. That was remarkable for a team that had won only 21 games the entire previous season. As the season progressed, Shaquille only got better. In a December game against the tough Utah Jazz, Shaq thundered his way to 28 points, 19 rebounds and 5 blocked shots, while the team continued its winning ways.

A real test for Shaquille and the Magic would come a few weeks later, however, when the division-leading New York Knicks came to town with center Patrick Ewing, regarded as one of the greatest centers ever to play the game. Ewing dazzled Shaquille with his agility and spin moves, sometimes making the rookie look confused. Ewing scored 17 points in the first three quarters as the Knicks built a 79–67 lead. But O'Neal and the Magic did not give up. The rookie scored 11 points alone in the fourth quarter and made a statement by blocking three of Ewing's shots in the quarter.

The Magic held a slim 1-point lead as the final seconds ticked away. Ewing grabbed the ball by the left baseline. He made a move to his left and then tried falling back for his trademark fadeaway jumper to win the game. But Shaq stuck with Ewing like glue and timed his jump perfectly to block Ewing's shot as the final buzzer sounded. The Magic won the game 95–94 and Shaquille O'Neal had come into his own.

Shaq was voted rookie of the year that season and was even the starting center for the all-star game ahead of Ewing. The Magic finished with a 41–41 record and just missed the playoffs. But great things were to come.

Meanwhile, Shaq began to enjoy his newfound wealth and fame. Sometimes, while driving around Orlando, Shaq would roll down his windows at red lights so that passengers in the cars near him could recognize him. He bought homes for his parents and both sets of grandparents. Then he set up a trust fund for his parents so that

> O'Neal proved himself to be one of the best centers in the NBA. He also made everyone else around him better.

they would never have to worry about money again. He has also been known to slip $100 bills into the pockets of homeless people sleeping on the streets. For himself? Shaq bought several cars and a mansion on the lake, had his own personal chef, and owned just about every video gaming system in existence.

The next season Shaq averaged 29.3 points and led the Magic to their first playoff appearance. Exactly one year later, Shaq would lead his team to the NBA finals by again averaging 29.3 points per game. Teaming up with point guard Anfernee Hardaway, the Magic looked unbeatable. That is, until they ran into the Houston Rockets in the finals.

Despite advantages in age, height, and sheer power, Shaquille was outplayed and overmatched by Houston center Hakeem Olajuwon. The Nigerian-born Olajuwon would use his experience and guile to a clear advantage. Still, before the series started, Hakeem said he was not looking forward to playing against the young center.

"My task is going to be big," Olajuwon said. "I'm jumping from the frying pan into the fire."[1]

The first game was in Orlando and it was a real battle. The Rockets overcame a 20-point deficit to win in overtime as Olajuwon jumped in front of Shaq to put in a tip-in shot at the buzzer. The crowd fell silent as the emotional game had slipped away from the Magic.

"It was so quiet that I didn't realize the basket went in," Olajuwon said of the stunned crowd.[2]

Shaq finished the game with 26 points and 16 rebounds, but it had not been enough. In Game 2, it seemed as if Orlando's spirit had been broken in the first game and the Rockets cruised to a 117–106 victory. In that game, Olajuwon proved himself to be

Shaq stands under the basket as Orlando teammate Penny Hardaway scores with the two-handed jam in October 1993.

braver than most NBA centers. He stood his ground defensively and drew a charging foul against Shaq as the 300-pounder slammed into him while going for a slam dunk.

The Rockets went on to sweep the series in four games for their second consecutive crown. But Shaquille and his teammates were proud of what they had accomplished and were looking for better things to come.

"This is our first time," said Shaquille, who averaged 28 points, 12.5 rebounds, and 6 assists for the series. "This is a learning experience. I'm going to get here again before I retire. I'm going to get here many times."[3]

Shaq's statement would prove true, though he would never get there again with the Orlando Magic.

In the meantime, America started seeing more and more of Shaq as he began pursuing secondary careers as an actor and rapper. He also began appearing in many television commercials for Allsport, Pepsi and Taco Bell. Shaq won many fans for his portrayal of a college basketball star in the film *Blue Chips*, and then starred in a Disney production called *Kazaam*, about a genie who befriends a small boy.

America was drawn to this gentle giant who seemed at home playing ball with children,

Shaq and Hakeem Olajuwon jump for the opening tip at the start of Game 3 of the NBA Finals on June 14, 1995.

signing autographs, or munching on his favorite food—cheeseburgers—at a fast food restaurant. He even became one of the first players to have his own Web site established where he could market his clothing line, recordings, movies and basketball career. "With this new technology we will be able to reach people all over the world," Shaq said. "I am excited to go online with basketball fans from around the globe."[4]

> "This is a learning experience. I'm going to get here [to the NBA finals] again. . . . I'm going to get here many times."
> —Shaquille O'Neal

Shaq also began doing a lot of things behind the scenes for his community. He started up a Shaqa-Claus program in Florida to raise money for Christmas toys for needy children. He also participates in Reading Is Fundamental, Starlight Children's Foundation, and Future Leaders Through Mentoring programs. He is a firm believer in giving back to the community, he has said, never forgetting that times were sometimes financially tough for him and his family while growing up.

In 1996, Shaquille O'Neal was named as one of the fifty greatest players in NBA history. Although Shaq's popularity had begun to rival that of the great Michael Jordan, he was unable to get his Magic past

Jordan's Bulls when they met up in the Eastern Conference Finals in 1996. That summer, Shaquille became a free agent, meaning that he could sign a contract to play wherever he wanted to.

He had to make a big decision. He loved the Orlando area and loved the Magic's fans, but he also wanted to be in a place where he could concentrate on his acting and rapping careers. In a stunning announcement, Shaquille told the public that he had signed a $120 million contract with the Los Angeles Lakers.

Shaq was going to Hollywood. But first, that summer, Shaq would take part in his second dream team experience. He was named one of the centers for the U.S. Olympic basketball team that would win the gold medal in Atlanta. Shaq had already served on the gold-medal–winning dream team that breezed through the World Championship of Basketball in Toronto, Canada, in 1994.

The Los Angeles Lakers—a franchise rich with history and championships, dating back to the franchise's days in Minneapolis, Minnesota—welcomed Shaq with open arms. The team had been without a winner since 1991, and Lakers fans were sure that Shaquille O'Neal would be the one to help the team reclaim championship glory.

Shaq muscles his way between Michael Jordan and Scottie Pippen during a playoff game on May 18, 1995.

That's how it looked at first, too. Shaq and the newly charged Lakers were riding high in first place at the end of January when he hyperextended his left knee, fracturing a bone. The Lakers dropped 12 of their next 28 games without Shaq and fell to fourth place.

When Shaq returned, the Lakers did not miss a beat. His first night back he scored a game-high 24 points and grabbed 11 rebounds. Two days later, Shaq nailed a baseline jumper at the buzzer to help beat the Utah Jazz, 100–98.

Shaq and the Lakers made the playoffs with a 56–26 record but were eliminated in the second round by the Jazz. Despite the injuries, Shaq finished the season averaging 26.2 points per game. In the 51 games that Shaq played, the Lakers were 38–13! He knew that things would only be getting brighter.

Shaq and his longtime girlfriend celebrated the birth of their daughter, Taahirah, and the release of his third movie, *Steel*, that year. Great things were happening for O'Neal on and off the court.

"I never dreamed I would be playing for the Lakers," he said. "When I was a kid I hardly had any self-esteem," he added, saying that kids picked on him all the time and that those doubters were what kept him motivated.[5]

Shaq shares a few words with Michael Jordan during a break in a game in March 1995.

The 1997–98 season started out as one of much promise for the Lakers and their fans, and the Shaq-led bunch did not disappoint. The team rattled off an impressive 61 victories after an 11–0 start.

Near the end of the season, the Lakers really turned it on as they got ready to make a run at the championship. The team won an incredible 22 of its last 25 games to start postseason play. In one of those wins, Shaq scored 50 points in a rout of New Jersey.

The team cruised through playoff series with Portland and Seattle to make it to the Western Conference finals. But the team went cold and were swept in a terrible effort against the Utah Jazz.

It seemed that with Shaquille O'Neal, the Lakers were getting better and kept moving closer to winning an NBA championship. So there were a lot of high expectations placed on the 1998–99 Lakers to go far. But that season, as fate would have it, the owners and players could not come to a new labor agreement and there was a lockout by the owners. This meant that no basketball would be played until a new deal was in place. Nearly the entire season was lost. It finally started in February and the teams played shorter schedules.

By now, the Lakers had a bona fide second all-star

After joining the U.S. basketball team for the World Championship Tournament in Toronto in 1994, Shaq went on to join the U.S. Olympic Team in 1996. Here, he backs into the post against Angola's David Dias during an Olympic tournament game on July 22, 1996.

on the team in guard Kobe Bryant. He was the perfect complement to Shaq, a player who could score from the outside as well as slash his way to the basket. Now, teams could not focus their defense entirely on stopping Shaq. Despite this, the Lakers started out only 6–6, and coach Del Harris was fired. Assistant coach Kurt Rambis was named coach for the remainder of the season. The Lakers finished with a 31–19 mark and were swept in four games by San Antonio in the Western Conference semifinals.

In the off-season, the Lakers hired Phil Jackson to coach the team. Jackson had won several NBA championships as a player for the New York Knicks and as head coach of Michael Jordan and the Chicago Bulls. Perhaps he would be the final piece of the puzzle necessary to bring a championship to O'Neal's Lakers.

6

GREATEST GAME

Shaquille knew that Coach Jackson had coached Michael Jordan, arguably the best player in the history of basketball. So Shaq worked hard in the off-season and came to training camp in great shape. He wanted to impress his new coach and finally be able to hoist a championship trophy over his head.

And even though O'Neal had proven himself to be one of the greatest players in the history of the game, there was still some question about his desire. Some even said that he would never win a championship.

But sportswriter Allen Barra defended him. "Fans have been expecting O'Neal to deliver since he came out of college," Barra wrote. "No NBA player in the modern game has been so consistently judged not by what he has actually done (which in Shaq's case has been considerable) but by what he was expected to do."[1]

Even though he was already a great player, O'Neal was ready to do whatever it took to win that NBA championship and silence his critics once and for all. He began the season with a vengeance, easily winning the NBA Player of the Month award for November, a month in which he averaged more than 28 points and 13 rebounds per game. He would also win the award in February and March, becoming the first player ever to win three in one season.

The coaching staff and players meshed well as the players bought into Jackson's triangle offense strategy. The team started out 25–5. Shaq liked the triangle offense as well. "I think it [the triangle offense] has been very, very effective for Phil Jackson and if done correctly can be a very dangerous offense," Shaq would later say.[2]

Jackson used the triangle offense when he was coaching the Bulls as well. The offense, which features a lot of ball movement and passing, is known for having three post-up positions, emphasizing scoring from the outside. This type of offense also makes it easier for the defense to get back and not allow any easy baskets.

Although the team was indeed playing great, there was a day in December that meant more to Shaq and his family than any slam dunk ever could. The big fella was excused from a game against the

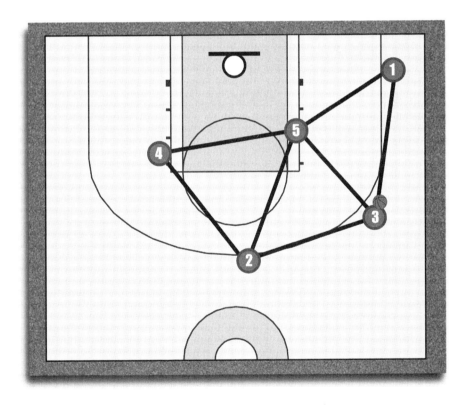

This diagram illustrates the "sideline triangle" of the triangle offense. The key to the offense is the spacing between the five players—if there is not enough space, defensive players can crowd and clog passing lanes. Ideally, all players should be athletic enough to handle any position of the triangle.

Vancouver Grizzlies so that he could attend his college graduation. It took longer than he had anticipated, but Shaq kept his promise to his family and earned his diploma by going to school part time while playing in the NBA.

"It didn't seem right to me to be telling kids to stay in school when I hadn't gotten my degree," Shaq said shortly after the ceremony. "Now I can tell them to stay in school."[3]

The new college graduate returned to the basketball court with a vengeance and helped lead the Lakers to the best record in the league that season: 67–15. This was important because it meant the Lakers would have the home court advantage for the entire playoffs. They would need it, especially in the first round when they needed five games to put away the pesky Sacramento Kings. They then disposed of the Phoenix Suns in five games before winning the Western Conference championship against the Portland Trail Blazers.

The Lakers were going to the 2000 NBA Finals against the Indiana Pacers. Most experts did not give Reggie Miller and the rest of the Indiana Pacers much of a chance against the powerful Lakers. And for the first two games of the series it looked as if they were right. Los Angeles cruised to easy victories in Games 1 and 2, winning 104–87 and 111–104. Indiana proved a bit tougher when they held off the Lakers 100–91 in Game 3, but then dropped an over-time heartbreaker to the Lakers in Game 4, 120–118. The resilient Pacers bounced back and swamped the Lakers in the next game, 120–87.

This set up a Game 6 showdown that the Lakers did not want to lose. Shaq described the night of the game as "the night I had been waiting for since I first picked up a ball as a five year old in Newark, New Jersey."[4]

It was clear from early on in the contest that the Pacers were a team that wanted to impose its will. They pushed the ball hard and fast against the Lakers, who seemed to be caught back on their heels as the Pacers opened up a quick 12-point lead. The Laker bench was no match for Indiana's Austin Croshere, who scored a quick 10 points early in the second quarter, and Sam Perkins added a pair of three-pointers. But that was when Shaq really went to work. He told his teammates that he would be camping out down at the low post

> "[It was] the night I had been waiting for since I first picked up a ball as a five year old in Newark, New Jersey."
>
> —Shaq on playing in Game 6 of the 2000 NBA Finals

Shaq prevents Indiana Pacers guard Reggie Miller from reaching the basket during Game 6 of the 2000 NBA Finals.

and that no one could stop him. A dunk, followed by a bank shot, another dunk on a put-back, and a soft short jumper on a feed from Kobe Bryant gave the Lakers life. Shaq scored 15 of his 21 first-half points in the second quarter just to keep the game fairly close.

But Jalen Rose and Reggie Miller were nearly unstoppable. They came out for the third quarter with even more confidence and determination than they had before. Their outside shooting and slashing toward the basket provided the answer every time the Lakers seemed ready to take the lead. Rose even ended the third quarter with an incredible seventeen-foot turnaround jumper that he somehow was able to float over Shaq's outstretched arms.

The Los Angeles crowd watched in silence as the Pacers kept the pressure on. But the fourth quarter belonged to the eight-year player with the big smile and the size twenty-three sneakers: Shaquille O'Neal. He made three consecutive baskets early in the period and was able to draw fouls on all three. Even though he did not convert the free throws, this was important because later in the game the Pacers would be over the foul limit and give the Lakers more opportunities at the charity stripe.

A few minutes later the Pacers were threatening

to pull away again when Shaq slammed down consecutive rebounds for dunks that brought the crowd to their feet. They could smell a championship. If the crowd was excited now, then they would raise the roof a few minutes later when the Lakers grabbed their first lead since very early in the game. Shaq ran the floor ahead of teammate Kobe Bryant, who led him with a perfect fast-break pass. Shaq banked the ball in before crashing to the floor as he was fouled from behind. The crowd went wild. The Lakers had taken a 91–90 lead.

From that moment on, Shaq was a rebounding machine and defensive presence in the paint as he thwarted one Pacer advance after another. Seconds before the final buzzer sounded, signifying a 116–111 victory and a Lakers championship, Shaquille O'Neal's eyes began to well with tears.

It was, arguably, Shaquille O'Neal's greatest game. Sure he has had games where he scored more points or grabbed more rebounds, but this was different. This time it was for the NBA championship. Almost singlehandedly, Shaq had willed his teammates to a championship. He had done what many of his critics said he would never be able to do. O'Neal had proven them wrong. By scoring 41 points and grabbing 12 rebounds, the man whose name means "Little Warrior" had played like a big warrior. His mother and sister ran onto the court and jumped up into his arms.

"This is my dream right here," Shaquille said as tears of joy streamed down his face. "This is what I wanted when I came to L.A. It's the only thing I play this game for."[5]

A few moments later, Shaquille held the league championship trophy high up over his head along with the series MVP trophy. He became only the third player in history to win the league most valuable player award, the all-star game MVP and the championship series MVP award in the same season.

Pacers coach and basketball legend Larry Bird said that the difference in the series was Shaquille O'Neal. "He's just so dominant," Bird

> "This is what I wanted when I came to L.A. It's the only thing I play this game for."
>
> —Shaquille O'Neal on winning his first championship.

said. "They [the Lakers] have a chance of doing something great for a number of years."[6]

When Shaq received his championship ring, he decided to give it to his father, Philip Harrison. "I might make myself a copy of my championship ring, but I will not keep the original," Shaq said. "It

Shaquille O'Neal is embraced by his father, Philip Harrison, after a playoff victory by the Lakers. Shaq gave his first championship ring to his father.

belongs to Philip. The next one I'll probably keep. But the first one is for him."[7]

It had been some year for Shaq. He graduated from college and won an NBA title. But the best was yet to come.

With the nucleus of Shaq, Kobe, and Coach Jackson returning for the 2000–01 season, there was a lot of optimism among Laker fans that the team could win back-to-back championships. But the club battled lots of injuries and by the all-star break had a record of only 31–16. This was more losses than they had totaled for the entire 1999–2000 season!

During the second half of the season, however, the Lakers got healthy and really started to pour it on. The season seemed to turn around during a come-from-behind, 96–88 victory over the Utah Jazz on April 3. The Lakers won their next eight games and beat out the up-and-coming Sacramento Kings for their second Pacific Division title. The Lakers were so hot that they swept through the first three rounds of the playoffs in series against Portland, Sacramento, and San Antonio, not losing a single game.

For the second straight year the Lakers were in the championship round. This time the opponent was the upstart Philadelphia 76ers, led by tenacious scorer Allen Iverson. In fact, it was Iverson who almost single-handedly took the first game, hitting a pair of clutch three-pointers as the Sixers took the opener in overtime.

However, although Iverson matched up well against Kobe Bryant, the Sixers had no answer for Shaquille O'Neal. Philadelphia had acquired defensive whiz Dikembe Mutombo in mid-season in an effort to keep Shaq away from the basket, but the younger, more athletic Shaq could not be stopped.

The Lakers won the next four games and Shaq was once again named MVP of the finals after averaging 33 points and 15.8 rebounds per game.

The 2001–02 season saw that same nucleus together and the Lakers once again steamrolled through the season, although it was clear that some teams in the West were starting to match up better with the Lakers. The Dallas Mavericks and the Sacramento Kings were two teams that had adapted a new style of run-and-gun basketball that featured big players who could dribble the basketball and shoot the three-pointer. More importantly, they were teams that could score bunches of points in a hurry and would be very dangerous.

The Kings, in fact, tallied the best record in the West and secured the home court advantage

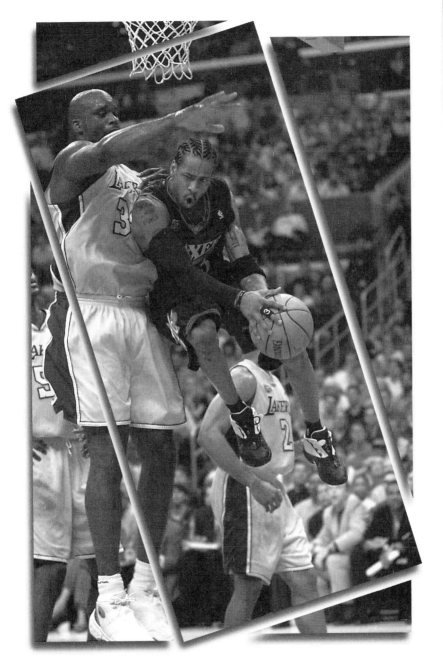

Shaq defends Allen Iverson of the Philadelphia 76ers during Game 1 of the 2001 NBA Finals.

for the playoffs. If the Lakers were to win a third championship in a row it would have to go through Sacramento. Shaq, although he was his usual dominating self when on the court, suffered through a series of nagging injuries that kept him off the court from time to time. The worst of the injuries was a constant foot pain that at one point had him even talking about retirement.

Still, even with a not-so-healthy Shaq in the middle, the Lakers, 58–24 in the regular season, would be hard to beat. They showed their playoff toughness during a series of easy victories against the Portland Trail Blazers and then the San Antonio Spurs. Even with the arthritic big-toe problem, Shaq proved to be unstoppable. Portland's Scottie Pippen was left shaking his head at Shaq's power. "When he wants to dunk the ball, there is no one who can stop him," Pippen said.[8]

The victory against the Spurs set up a matchup against the tough Sacramento Kings, led by Chris Webber. The Kings took the Lakers to seven games in a classic series, but once again the Lakers prevailed and would be going to their third NBA Finals in a row.

The Lakers were going up against the self-proclaimed team of destiny, the New Jersey Nets. The upstart Nets, led by flashy point guard Jason

Shaq takes a swipe at the ball as Chris Webber drives to the basket during a playoff game against the Sacramento Kings in June 2002.

Kidd, shocked the basketball world all season to make it this far. For Shaquille O'Neal, the opportunity to play New Jersey for a championship was a very special one.

"I was born and raised in Newark," he said. "Being from Newark made me who I am. . . . That's where I got my style from, being hard, being myself. If I wasn't from Jersey, I wouldn't be me."[9]

Shaq and the Lakers started out strong in the first two games of the series in Los Angeles. After the second game of the series had ended, the Nets were openly wondering if there was any way in the world to keep Shaq from scoring. He scored 40 points that game on six dunks, 12 free throws, and an array of soft jumpers and baby hook shots. He was indeed a complete scoring center.

"He's just such a dominating player," said Nets Head Coach Byron Scott. "I don't know what to do against Shaq."[10]

Back in New Jersey for Game 3, Shaq would play before many family members and old friends. He was determined to play his best in front of all of them and he did just that, lighting up Nets center Todd MacCulloch for 9 points in the game's first seven minutes. By game's end, teammate Kobe Bryant had poured in 36 points on 14 of 23 shooting to help lead

Shaq tries to block the shot of the Nets' Jason Kidd during Game 3 of the 2002 NBA Finals.

the Lakers to a 106–103 victory. This left L.A. just one game away from completing the sweep and taking home their third straight championship.

In the middle of the night right before Game 4, Shaq sneaked out to pay a secret visit to Weequahic Park in Newark, where he had played basketball as a young boy. "As a youngster, I used to play [there] with the raggedy basketball my father got me," Shaq would later say. "I used to dream about certain things. I stuck with it and all my dreams have come true. . . . I got my toughness in Brick City, going to the park, getting beat up [on the court] and my father and grandfather telling me to go back out there and fight."[11]

Shaq and the Lakers went on to win that fourth game and complete the sweep. The big center from nearby Newark, New Jersey, averaged 36.3 points per game for the series as the Lakers took home their third consecutive title. And for the third year in a row, Shaq was named the series MVP. After the big win, Shaq's family and friends swarmed the court to congratulate him.

"These days are some of the proudest in my life," Shaquille's grandfather, Donald Harrison, said as he stood on the court. "I've never been so happy as to see [Shaquille] grow up to be a man, a very gentle

Shaquille O'Neal holds the NBA championship trophy while his grandfather, Donald Harrison, proudly looks on, shortly after the Lakers completed their sweep of the New Jersey Nets in the 2002 NBA Finals.

giant. He is good for the game, he is good for the sport, and he is good for all the young people."[12]

Winning three championships in a row can take a toll, however. Shaq's big toe was hurting, and on September 11, 2002, he had surgery on it. This meant he would miss the start of the 2002–2003 season. By the time Shaq returned, the Lakers had lost 9 of the 12 games they had played without him. The team had to fight just to make the fifth seed of the playoffs. And although they managed to defeat the fourth-seeded Minnesota Timberwolves in the first round, the Lakers were eliminated in the second round by the San Antonio Spurs, four games to two.

The Lakers responded by adding big-name veterans Gary Payton and Karl Malone for the 2003–2004 season. This helped propel the team all the way back to the NBA Finals. But the team lost in a surprising upset to the Detroit Pistons in just five games. This led to much speculation about the future of Shaquille O'Neal. It was widely rumored that he and Kobe Bryant had been battling over team leadership and that the two could no longer play together.

In July, Shaq began a new chapter in his career when he was traded to the Miami Heat. At a press conference in Miami he stated: "When I was looking for cities to come to, Miami was one of my choices for one reason. . . . I saw that they were just a great team and I just wanted to be part of a team, because I know in basketball you can't do it by yourself, no matter how great you are or . . . think you are."[13]

Shaq made his intentions in Miami very clear. "I am just coming here to bring a championship to this city," he said.[14]

CHAPTER
NOTES

Chapter I. No Pressure at All

1. Bruce Hunter, *Shaq Impaq* (Chicago: Bonus Books, 1993), p. 272.
2. Ibid., p. 273.

Chapter 2. Little Warrior

1. Bruce Hunter, *Shaq Impaq* (Chicago: Bonus Books, 1993), p. 109.
2. Ibid., p. 109.
3. "Shaquille O'Neal," *The Basketball Man*, n.d., <http://www.angelfire.com/la/BasketballMan/shaqslife.html> (May 1, 2003).

Chapter 3. A Basketball Future

1. Bruce Hunter, *Shaq Impaq* (Chicago: Bonus Books, 1993), p. 110.
2. Ibid., p. 111.
3. "SportsLine goes one on one with Shaq," *Shaq World Online*, December 18, 2000, <http://cbs.sportsline.com/u/fans/celebrity/shaq/forum/qa.html> (May 1, 2003).
4. Hunter, p. 113.

Chapter 4. College Superstar

1. Neil Cohen, *Sports Illustrated for Kids: Shaquille O'Neal* (New York: Bantam Books, 1993), p. 35.
2. Bruce Hunter, *Shaq Impaq* (Chicago: Bonus Books, 1993), p. 119.

3. Cohen, p. 43.

4. Ibid.

5. Ibid., p. 55.

Chapter 5. NBA Stardom

1. Robert Falkoff, "Hakeem's American Dream," *The Sporting News 1989-90 Pro Basketball Yearbook* (St. Louis: The Sporting News Publishing Co., 1989), p. 62.

2. Roland Lazenby, *The NBA Finals: A Fifty Year Celebration* (New York: Masters Press, 1996), p. 315.

3. Ibid.

4. "Shaquille O'Neal Takes His Game to the World Wide Web," June 26, 1996, <www.about.sportsline.com/release/shaq.htm> (September 1, 2002).

5. Rick Reilly, "Shaq's World," *Sports Illustrated*, April 21, 1997, p. 89.

Chapter 6. Greatest Game

1. Allen Barra, "With this Ring Shaq Emerges," *Salon.com*, June 2, 2000, <http://www.salon.com/news/feature/2000/06/02/shaq/> (May 1, 2003).

2. "Chat Live With Shaq!" *Shaq World Online*, March 21, 2001, <http://cbs.sportsline.com/u/fans/celebrity/shaq/forum/chat.html> (May 1, 2003).

3. Jimmy Traina, "Shaquille O'Neal Scrapbook: Timeline," *CNNSI.com - SI Online*, January 3, 2002, <http://sportsillustrated.cnn.com/basketball/nba/feature/shaq/timeline> (May 1, 2003).

4. Shaquille O'Neal, *Shaq Talks Back* (New York: St. Martin's Press, 2001), p. 1.

5. Associated Press, "Lakers Put Pacers away in Game 6 to win NBA Title," June 19, 2000.

6. Mike Lopresti, "Lakers Overcome Indiana in Game 6," *USA Today*, Gannett News Service, June 20, 2000.

7. Shaquille O'Neal, *Shaq Talks Back*, p. 259.

8. David DuPree, "L.A. Shows Mettle," *USA Today*, April 29, 2002, p. C1.

9. Dave D'Alessandro, "Made in Jersey," *Newark Star-Ledger* (New Jersey), February 16, 2003, section 5, p. 12.

10. Associated Press; "Lakers Ride Shaq to 2–0 Series Lead Against Nets," June 8, 2002.

11. Steve Wilstein, "Lakers Become One of All-Time Greats," Associated Press, June 14, 2002.

12. "Cutting Down the Nets," *CNNSI.com*, June 13, 2002, <http://sportsillustrated.cnn.com/basketball/nba/2002/playoffs/news/2002/06/12/lakers_nets_ap> (May 1, 2003).

13. "Shaquille O'Neal Press Conference," *NBA.com*, n.d., <http://www.nba.com/heat/news/oneal_presser_040720.html> (August 24, 2004).

14. Ibid.

CAREER STATISTICS

COLLEGE

Season	Team	GP	FG%	REB	PTS	PPG
1989–90	LSU	32	.573	385	445	13.9
1990–91	LSU	28	.628	411	774	27.6
1991–92	LSU	30	.615	421	722	24.1
Totals		90	.610	1,217	1,941	21.6

GP—Games Played **REB**—Rebounds **BLK**—Blocks
FG%—Field Goal **AST**—Assists **PTS**—Points
    Percentage **STL**—Steals **PPG**—Points Per Game

NBA

Season	Team	GP	FG%	REB	AST	STL	BLK	PTS	PPG
1992–93	Orlando	81	.562	1,122	152	60	286	1,893	23.4
1993–94	Orlando	81	.599	1,072	195	76	231	2,377	29.3
1994–95	Orlando	79	.583	901	214	73	192	2,315	29.3
1995–96	Orlando	54	.573	596	155	34	115	1,434	26.6
1996–97	L.A. Lakers	51	.557	640	159	46	147	1,336	26.2
1997–98	L.A. Lakers	60	.584	681	142	39	144	1,699	28.3
1998–99	L.A. Lakers	49	.576	525	114	36	82	1,289	26.3
1999–00	L.A. Lakers	79	.574	1,078	299	36	239	2,344	29.7
2000–01	L.A. Lakers	74	.572	940	277	47	204	2,125	28.7
2001–02	L.A. Lakers	67	.579	715	200	41	137	1,822	27.2
2002–03	L.A. Lakers	67	.574	742	206	38	159	1,841	27.5
2003–04	L.A. Lakers	67	.584	769	196	34	166	1,439	21.5
Totals		809	.577	9,781	2,309	560	2,102	21,914	27.1

WHERE
TO WRITE

Mr. Shaquille O'Neal
c/o Miami Heat
American Airlines Arena
601 Biscayne Blvd.
Miami, FL 33132

INTERNET ADDRESSES

Shaquille O'Neal: Official Site of BBallOne.com

http://www.bballone.com/shaqo/shaquilleoneal.
  html

Shaquille O'Neal Player Page

http://sportsillustrated.cnn.com/basketball/nba/
  players/847/

The Official Site of the Miami Heat

http://www.nba.com/heat/

INDEX